SECRETS
of the
MOORS & DALES

Left: *Alum Pot*

SECRETS

of the

MOORS & DALES

John and Eliza Forder

FRANK PETERS

PUBLISHING

Acknowledgements

We felt drawn to work in the North York Moors partly because we wanted to photograph a different landscape and people, and also because it allowed us to record an aspect of rural life that we had not documented before. Our knowledge about the upkeep of heather moorland, its links with sporting interests, and the work of gamekeepers was limited, so we were able to embark upon the project with relatively few preconceived notions.

Both of us made every effort to ignore reports and anecdotes we had heard about gamekeepers, for we wanted to discover the truth about their work for ourselves. In retrospect we found that many stories we had heard bore little resemblance to reality, and we soon realised that judgments based on ignorance can create prejudice and cause a lot of harm. In SECRETS OF THE MOORS & DALES we have attempted to tell the story of the moor as we found it, and have made every effort to be as objective as possible.

We followed a gamekeeper throughout the seasons of the year making every attempt to question and understand the nature of his work. We soon recognized that he had a deep love and respect for the moor and its wildlife, and saw that his main concern was to see this unique habitat survive. We also learned that if the heather moorland is to flourish it needs careful management and, undoubtedly, it is the gamekeepers who perform this task. Nowadays it seems that conservationists as well as ornithologists are beginning to realise the valuable role that gamekeepers perform.

We are especially grateful to Neil Radcliffe, game-keeper of Rosedale Moor, for the trust and friendship he showed us at a time when many gamekeepers were apprehensive about welcoming strangers. Neil assisted us in every way possible and allowed us to accompany him during his daily routine whenever we wished. We would also like to express our appreciation to his estate manager, Robert Holmes, and to members of the Rosedale shoot, who showed interest in our work and always made us feel welcome. Without their support we could not have made this book.

We are grateful to Sue Rees, the ecologist at the National Park, who kept us advised and informed on many issues regarding conservation, and also helped by arranging contacts for us. Similarly we would like to extend our gratitude to John Mackenzie, the district manager for the Forestry Commission, who took time in explaining and showing us the different aspects of forestry work. We would also like to thank Richard David for once again editing the text, and the farmers of Bransdale and Farndale whose sense of humour brightened up many a visit to the moors!

Lastly we would like to acknowledge our publishers and printers, Frank Peters, who take great trouble in reproducing our photographs to an exceptionally high standard. This involves a team of dedicated people who work on our pictures from the design stage, right through to the careful supervision of the images reeling off the four-colour presses. As photographers we rely on this complex process of reproduction for accurate results, and we owe much to Frank Peters for their skill and care. We are particularly indebted to the firm's managing director, Colin Baker, whom we are fortunate to have as our sympathetic and supportive publisher.

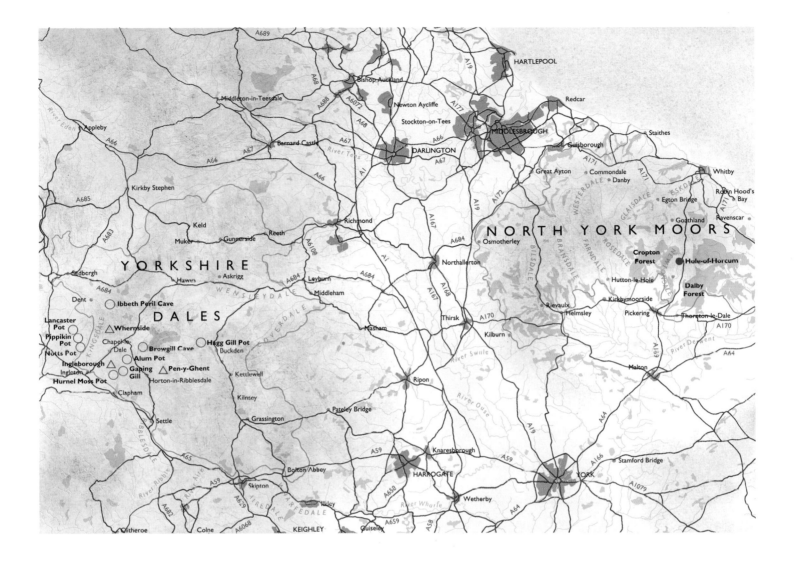

KEY

Roads	——————
Rivers	~~~~~~
Woodland	▬▬▬
Pots	○
Peaks	△
National Park Boundary	———————

Red Grouse

The Open Moors

As the sun's rays break through the threatening clouds the light catches the moorland tops and, what before seemed a never-ending sea of purple and grey-green, suddenly takes on shape and form. The continuous stretch of heather separates out and is transformed into a myriad different clumps, the subtle contours of the moor become defined, and an ancient way-marker and well-worn track provide direction where before there was none.

The numerous dales that intersect the moor do little to interrupt the feeling of expanse and openness. Though each dale creates its own pattern and character, none is so deeply carved as to suggest any sense of enclosure or restriction. The North York Moors, one of the finest areas of true heather moorland left in Great Britain, is a wide open landscape that inspires and uplifts both those who work there, and those who visit.

This large block of land, made up of numerous individual moors merging one into another, stretches from the coast in the east to the Vale of York in the west. It is a place where the abundance of low vegetation affords little protection from the weather and so the intruder can feel exposed to the elements. The stunted birch, the odd pine tree, offer scant shelter on a winter's night when sleet and strong winds drive across the tops with no reprieve. Yet, although this land can feel wild, it is no wilderness. It is a land that is managed and looked after. Without this care, the heather moorland that celebrates its survival by

Bransdale

carpeting the tops in mauves and purply-pinks during August and September, might be threatened by change.

The moorland scenery has inspired poets and painters, writers and ramblers and yet, if it is to continue to flourish, it is in need of understanding by those who seek fulfilment from it. Inadvertently, harm can be done by those who fail to recognize the intricate balance of interests that is at the heart of moorland life. Since the nineteenth century, it has been the sporting interests that have enabled much of the moorland to survive because, if the grouse are to breed successfully, a programme of heather management is needed. Until the recent past, much of the open moor had disappeared with the spread of forestry and farming. But times have changed and this is no longer so. Increasingly the gamekeeper, forester, farmer and conservationist are working together so that the different strands of moorland life are able to co-exist harmoniously.

Heather has not always dominated the landscape. The scenery that we know today has evolved over the past million years as a result of the last Ice Age. Three glaciers converged on the district from the North Sea, Scotland and the Lake District and, although these were not thick enough to cover the moorland tops, they exerted their influence in the valleys. The ice finally melted in a thaw that began twenty thousand years ago and, as it departed, the shifting glaciers left in their wake the dales, gorges and hills, as well as a number of lakes that have long since drained away. The vale of Pickering which now hums to the sound of farm machinery is, in fact, the fertile bed of what may have been the largest lake in England.

After the ice had gone, the first significant vegetation that appeared was scrub consisting mainly of birch and juniper intermixed with some pine. The shelter provided by these trees allowed oak, hazel and elm to gain a hold and, as the climate warmed, the whole area soon became covered by dense forest. Paradoxically, within two thousand years of the ice disappearing, the climate was much warmer and drier than it is today, and it was around this time that man sought refuge among the moors.

The primitive hunters, in search of game, migrated to the higher ground which was less densely forested. As trees were felled to be used for shelter, heating and cooking, land clearance began and it was not long before

Dalby Forest

there was sufficient open ground to grow crops and graze animals. As reminders of this distant past a large number of burial grounds, or tumuli, belonging to ancient chieftains can be found scattered around the moors.

These first inhabitants soon realized that after a few years of growing crops on thin, sandy soils, the land was rendered useless and they had to move on. As a result of this constant movement of people, the higher ground gradually became denuded of trees and devoid of nutrients, and the vegetation began to change: heather slowly colonized the moor. By the time the Saxons, Danes and Vikings had arrived around the ninth and tenth centuries, the climate was no longer as kind as it had been to these first settlers. Consequently this later wave of invaders were forced to clear the valley woodland, recognizing that the lower lands would provide more shelter. Small hamlets were set up in carefully chosen sites close to rivers and springs, and village communities started to grow.

Swaledale sheep – Westerdale Moor

During this time the spread of Christianity was also having a marked effect upon the region. Religious foundations were set up and, despite persecution from both the Vikings and the Normans, abbeys and monastic orders became a vital part of the local economy. Although some domestic animals had grazed the moorland since the forest was first cleared, it was the monks who made a thriving industry from creating vast sheep-runs. Remaining woodland was cleared, barren land improved, and Rievaulx Abbey managed at one time to keep as many as fourteen thousand sheep on the moors near Ryedale and Bilsdale. The monks were not just successful farmers but good traders too, and they sold much of their wool to the cloth merchants of Europe.

As trade routes became better established, villages around the moorland edge became busy market towns: traders from the moors wanted cereals in exchange for their wool and meat. Waymarkers in the form of crosses were put up along the moorland tracks, serving as a reminder of Christ and a comfort to travellers on their way. The moor could be a bleak, inhospitable place for those crossing it in inclement weather.

The only major visual change that occurred after this was due to the enclosure of land during the seventeenth and eighteenth centuries. This left in its wake the familiar pattern of stone walls that now divide up the valley land.

So, whether it is walls or waymarkers, forest or ancient burial mounds, the purple heather or the Swaledale sheep, all can be seen as signs and symbols of our moorland past. Nowadays there is no single aspect that dominates life on the North York Moors – it is a balance that is sought between the different traditions and different expectations of those who use and enjoy them. This is a place where some seek solitude while others strive to make a living. It feels untamed yet it is a landscape that needs to be cared for. Above all, it is a fragile ecosystem in need of protection and understanding.

"The job of a grouse moor keeper is to provide a suitable habitat where these wild game birds can breed in peace. And then, if the moor is managed well, the grouse breed a surplus so that there are sufficient to shoot. But mind, that's no easy thing to do! They fly fast and low . . . and when you see them, there's an awful lot of room about them. They're an easy thing to miss!"

It is the gamekeepers who look after the heather moorland. They are employed by either a landowner or leaseholder and, in return for a cottage and modest income, they manage and protect the land so that the grouse can breed and rear their young successfully. During the autumn certain days are set aside on each moor, when a party of eight or nine 'guns' come to shoot the surplus birds. In this way, during winter and the following spring, the moor reverts to harbouring a comfortable number of grouse. If there are too many, diseases such as strongylosis, which is caused by a type of worm, can quickly spread among the birds wiping out vast numbers.

In the past gamekeepers have been put under much pressure by their patrons to ensure as good a crop of grouse as possible. This encouraged excessive control of predators in order to avoid losing too many chicks; it seemed that any threat by bird or small mammal had to be promptly dealt with. But nowadays landowners have become more tolerant and increasingly aware of environmental concerns, and they acknowledge that a balance has to be maintained on the moor. If that means fewer grouse and fewer shooting days, then so be it.

"We're all a more enlightened lot these days," explains the gamekeeper, "and if I can boast of nesting merlin, short-eared owl, curlew, golden plover and numbers of waders on my moor, that makes me a proud keeper. Everyone likes to see a range of bird life, and if moorland is well-keepered it can help to support that."

And there seems little doubt that there are many species of birds, apart from the grouse, that benefit from managed moorland.

One of the main tasks of a keeper is to ensure that there is a mosaic of differently aged heathers. Grouse prefer the older, taller heather for nesting cover while the younger, more nutritious shoots get taken for feed. When the heather is about ten years old, it starts to degenerate, losing its value to grouse as well as to sheep. At this stage the gamekeeper sets it alight and burns off sufficient to leave as little stalk or 'cowling' as possible. A clean burn stimulates new growth among the charred remains. Ideally the aim is to create a patchwork of heathers at various stages of growth over the whole moor, so that the grouse have some choice in their particular territory.

A gamekeeper

"Grouse like to nest just a little way in from the edge of a burn. That way they have good cover for their eggs, but the chicks are able to get out to clearer ground when they're ready. If grouse nest in a jungle of old heather, the young birds get lost and find it difficult to get away."

Although grouse like bilberries and seeds from the cotton grass, they feed principally on ling heather. They are highly selective feeders and will only take the most nutritious shoots of three or four years old. But heather is not easy to digest and grouse need a certain amount of grit in their gizzards to help them grind it down. On peat moors, where this is not available naturally, the keeper has to provide it for them.

Grouse also need water and, where the moor is dry, the keeper may have to create artificial ponds which help to attract waders and other birds. Although insects found in wet areas make vital food for grouse chicks, if the moor is too boggy the keeper may have to devise means of draining it to prevent the heather from getting waterlogged. It is in this way that he manages the moorland, so that the grouse can thrive in their own environment.

The main hazard for grouse comes from predators who see their eggs and chicks as easy prey. The young birds have little chance of survival unless there is some control over the foxes and crows that are about during the breeding season. Other ground nesting birds also benefit when some degree of protection is afforded them.

"Weeding! That's what it's called. You have to weed your garden otherwise there wouldn't be a lot of grouse about. And it's this job that has given gamekeepers a bad name. Today no poison should ever be used and, if there's a gamekeeper who breaks that rule, he's making bad trouble for us all. Nowadays we use tunnel traps and these kill predators such as stoats, weasels and mink instantaneously. Larsen traps are used for the magpies and crows and, as for the foxes, we either shoot them at night with a high powered rifle, or set snares for them."

It is a familiar track that the gamekeeper follows each day across the moor during winter and springtime, checking each trap and re-baiting when necessary. On occasion he will use his ferret to bolt rabbits or his terrier to bolt foxes, but for the most part he will rely upon his traps to do the work. After a sharp frost or a snowfall, he will be out early to check for footprints as these provide the most valuable source of information as to what animals are about. Until early summer, when the breeding season has finished, a conscientious gamekeeper will be vigilant in watching over his young.

On the North York Moors shooting does not usually begin until late August, when the young birds are strong enough to fly fast. A shoot provides a welcome opportunity for people to come together for a day out;

they love to work their dogs, breathe in the moorland air, listen to news from different dales and also earn some pocket money. The moorland echoes to the vibrant sounds of local life and culture.

The gamekeeper may need thirty or more beaters to raise the grouse in the direction of the shooting butts, and he will rely upon his friends and village folk to help out. He takes into consideration the direction of the wind and the particular terrain of each drive, and arranges his team of beaters and flankers accordingly. Then, like advancing infantry, the beaters start to move forward waving their flags while trying to maintain as steady a line as possible. At the same time each man will try to watch out for treacherous ditches, holes and bogs that remain concealed underneath the profusion of heather. It is not unusual to tumble.

Some birds fly up only to settle down again, others fly away from the butts or out to one side, and just a few get driven on towards the guns. The beaters work up a sweat as they push their way through the patches of overgrown heather, lifting their legs high to avoid the woody clumps. It is hard work and many miles are covered in a morning, but the day is filled with an air of excitement and exhilaration and weariness is slow to set in. As the beaters move close to the butts, the gamekeeper's whistle sounds out across the moor, indicating the end of another drive.

Great care is taken to retrieve all the birds for although the majority are killed outright, there may be the odd one with an injury that needs putting out of its misery. Despite the emotional reaction about shooting birds – largely by people who live away from the moors – local opinion holds that this wild game bird has a good life on the heather moor, until it either dies naturally or is shot . . . and many a bird is missed! How different from the lives of farm animals and fowl, which are subjected to endless procedures for disease control, are often kept in confined housing, and then have to suffer slaughter

Beaters on a shoot

in places that surely are tainted with the smell of death. As one beater said, "I would sooner be a red grouse enjoying a fine bit of heather moorland . . . anytime . . ."

No-one doubts that it is the sporting interests that have helped to ensure the survival of the heather moorland. Over the years about twenty per cent of the North York Moors has been converted to extensive areas of forest. There were major programmes of afforestation after the First and Second World Wars, when it was recognized that there was an urgent need for more timber, and land could be bought very cheaply. Nowadays it is accepted that large, uniform plantations of conifers lack the diversity to support a range of wildlife; but these trees were planted solely in order to replenish the country's depleted timber reserves as quickly as possible.

Now that many of these earlier plantations have reached maturity, it is possible to re-afforest in a way that is both ecologically and aesthetically more in line with current environmental policies. Woodland management needs vision and sensitive planning, in the same way that heather moorland does. The forest is a constantly evolving habitat, and the older it gets the more chance there is of creating areas of natural beauty that are rich in wildlife. The forester now has the responsibility not only of providing a sustainable timber resource, but also of improving the environment by setting appropriate conservation and recreational standards.

This can be achieved in a number of ways. Although conifers have to be planted close to one another for economic viability, the forest can be landscaped to minimize the effects of uniformity. Whereas felling normally takes place when trees are about fifty years old, some Scots pine are now being left to reach full maturity. When this occurs the trees assume their true magnificence and, as the canopy becomes higher and less dense, more

A 'gun' takes aim at a grouse

light filters through allowing spontaneous regeneration to take place. This helps to create islands of natur-alness in the forest.

Along road sides and streams, trees are being deliberately taken out haphazardly to help break up the monotony of the plantation edge. And, within the forest itself, different conifers such as Sitka spruce, larch, Scots pine, Douglas fir and Norway spruce are intermixed to bring about a mosaic of colour and shape.

If the trees in a plantation vary both in species and in age, there is more likelihood that different forms of wildlife will flourish. Mature and dead wood provide habitat and food for fungi, lichens, butterflies and other insects, and also make good nesting sites for birds and bats. Broad-leaved trees, such as oak, beech, birch and sycamore are either planted or left to re-seed naturally on the more fertile slopes in the valley bottoms. Occasionally conifers are mixed with slower growing broadleaves, such as sycamore and oak, in order to 'nurse' them along. As the conifers mature they are felled, allowing the woodland to become a broad-leaved habitat.

Although little sunlight reaches the forest floor in a planted coniferous woodland, the larch has a light, deciduous foliage which allows some ground flora to develop. As the trees grow taller and are thinned, woodland plants and flowers are able to set seed. By contrast with the evolving forest, the verges of the roads and rides become permanent sanctuaries for wild flowers. In some of these sites a more diverse flora can be supported, including a variety of orchids such as common spotted, early purple, twayblade and fragrant.

Within the forest itself, specific wetland habitats have been intentionally left unplanted, so that they become havens where sphagnum mosses, marsh marigold, bog asphodel and rarer plants such as grass of Parnassus can

Paradise Wood

remain undisturbed. Management of these open spaces also helps to increase the conservation value of the forest as years go by.

Alongside the upkeep of the heather moorlands and the management of the forests, farming also plays a crucial part in the life of the moor. Like the forester and gamekeeper, the farmer is increasingly regarded as an important custodian of the environment. As livelihoods are threatened by falling sheep prices and the inherent problems of farming marginal land, grant-aided schemes that encourage sensitive management are being welcomed. The North York Moors National Park has been instrumental in giving financial support to farmers who are willing to lay hedges, repair walls, protect areas of woodland, and limit the use of fertilizers on unimproved grassland and hay meadows.

Much of the land within the National Park is owned either by private landowners or the Forestry Commission. One of the main tasks of the Park Authority is to try to reconcile the varied interests that fall within its boundaries. As well as those who make their living from the moor, there are the many visitors who flock to the area each year and their needs have to be accommodated too.

"Serious walkers, as such, do no harm – only problem comes when they lose their way because footpaths are badly marked, but they're happy to be set right," explains a gamekeeper. "What I find causes most upset is when folk come and park up – out with the dogs, out with the kids, all over the bloody place! Poor birds don't stand a chance. No ground nesting bird likes to be disturbed. If there's a well-trod footpath, the birds soon learn to nest away, but if folk just wander anywhere, the birds can't get any peace."

Throughout the seasons of the year the 'ge-bak, ge-bak' of the grouse serves as a reminder that the heather is both their nesting and feeding ground and their call acts as a warning to intruders. The landowners and gamekeepers are naturally concerned about potential disturbance to nesting chicks. Unleashed dogs cause havoc: they can kill young birds and devastate nests just for fun, unlike the fox who kills to eat.

A compromise has to be reached if the requirements of the landowners and the wishes of the visitors are both to be met. To roam among the heather may be the

Winter feeding

instinctive desire of a city-dweller, but there needs to be mutual understanding and respect if everyone is to reap benefit from the moor.

Another responsibility of the National Park is to promote and encourage conservation within its boundaries, initiating research projects where they can. When, in 1976, a large area of moorland was devastated by fire, the heather was completely destroyed because the peat burned underground for several days. In response, different methods were tried to help bring the heather back quickly. Heather, cut from a nearby moor, was laid out on the bare peat surface in the hope that its seeds would take hold before blowing away. Fencing was also put up to prevent sheep from grazing new shoots. Within six years the project proved successful, and now there is increased confidence that even on an area of barren moorland, where erosion from wind and rain is at its greatest, heather can re-colonize.

The Park Authority also seeks agreement with landowners and tenants as to how the land can best be looked after to benefit the environment. If a landowner wishes to conserve and enhance an area of broad-leaved woodland, the National Park is able to help with the cost of protective fencing and extra planting. The project may not immediately benefit the owner, but the environment will gain as the years go by. In the same way farmers may be given financial help to make such improvements to their land and buildings as will benefit the Park. The extra money is a valuable addition to the farm income and allows the farmer to manage with fewer sheep. If there are too many animals on the moor, the result is over-grazing which can be detrimental to the heather.

There are other concerns, such as the control of bracken, that affect all those who have an interest in the moor. Bracken has little to offer sheep, grouse or the walker, and it insidiously encroaches upon the moorland. Consequently a bracken control programme has been initiated and ways of encouraging alternative forms of vegetation are being tried out. In some places it is hoped that the heather will come back, otherwise the land may revert to traditional pasture or be planted with broad-leaved trees. Another possibility is that the original scrub woodland of rowan, birch and oak may once again be able to take hold along the moorland edges through a

Ralph Cross

programme of planting and regeneration. The idea is to blend together the different forms of vegetation that have been prevalent on the moors for thousands of years.

Much thought has gone into balancing the moorland ecology and it seems that, if each interest is protected sympathetically, then the environment gains. No-one doubts that it is the shooting interests that finance the upkeep of heather moorland but, if gamekeepers do their work with sensitivity, then other forms of bird life can flourish alongside the grouse. Similarly in the dales, it is the farmers who have to be relied upon to look after the valley land by promoting good pasture, managing hedges and repairing walls. Within the forests, it is the responsibility of the managers to ensure that there are enough trees of different species and ages to enhance the scenery and stimulate a diversity of wildlife.

The North York Moors have evolved over thousands of years and their various aspects reflect a rich history. Within Britain is contained half the heather moorland of the world and it would be a tragedy if this heritage were to be reduced further.

It is a landscape of wild beauty and serenity and, when the sweep of purple stretches out across the hills, we are reminded that this place has a splendour all of its own. As the autumn sun sinks lower in the sky, and catches the heather with its slanting light, each petal and leaf is picked out, and the essence of the moor is captured. This image persists in the memory.

Ling Heather

19

Red grouse

Sunrise over Bransdale

The North York Moors extend to the sea in the east –
view down Glaisdale

The Hole of Horcum
The bare ground is the result of a bracken spraying programme which has been initiated to help the heather grow back

Heather and bilberry above Farndale
Although grouse feed principally on ling heather, bilberry also plays an important part in their diet

The heather moor supports sheep as well as grouse – Bransdale

Neil Radcliffe – gamekeeper of Rosedale Moor

The job of the gamekeeper is to care for the heather moorland.
Picking up litter and spent cartridges from around the shooting butts

Left: *Fat Betty*
The moor is divided into different estates and this stone represents the meeting point between Rosedale,
Westerdale and Danby

In Bransdale, where the moor is too dry, keeper Colin Short supervises the digging of several ponds which will benefit not just grouse and sheep, but also waders and other birds

After only a year one of the new ponds blends in with the environment, as mosses and other plants take advantage of the wetter habitat

One of the gamekeeper's jobs is to control the predators that take grouse eggs and chicks. Checking a trap above Northdale prior to setting it beneath a boulder

Top left: *Sometimes it's too dry and sometimes it's too wet!*
Where the moor is boggy, drainage channels have to be kept clear
Bottom left: *It falls to the keeper to warn the public when there is a fire risk*

A terrier pup – when older it will be trained up to bolt foxes

Left: Experience dictates the best place to put a trap. A tunnel trap is built into a wall in the knowledge that stoat and mink are likely to be channelled into it

From January until summer time the gamekeeper follows a familiar
track across the moor each day to check and re-bait his traps –
Rosedale Moor

A hungry Swaledale tup

When the mists come down the moors become a bleak place –
Farndale

Feeding sheep in Bransdale

A forest ride near Sutton Bank

During the winter the old heather is set alight in a carefully planned programme of burning

The fire is kept under control by beating

New shoots grow up through the charred remains

Left: The direction of the wind is assessed so that the fire can be driven to a natural break, such as a wall or stream, where it burns itself out

A good proportion of the moors has now been converted to forestry.
Planting larch trees on clear felled land –
three people working together move along in lines, to ensure even
spacing between the trees

A young plantation where both broad-leaved trees and conifers have been mixed together – Bickley

Sometimes trees are taken out to allow more light to filter through the canopy, so that natural regeneration can take place

Overleaf: At Keldy an area of the forest is left undisturbed in order to encourage wildlife. A Canada goose nests on the central island

Detail of the forest floor

Lambing time in Bransdale

Wild daffodils – Farndale

Detail of larch tree – a deciduous conifer

In Newtondale different species of trees are intermixed to help break up the uniformity of the forest

A plantation of Scots pine – Dalby Forest

Beech tree

When 'natural' forest conditions are simulated and native species are included, the area becomes more valuable to wildlife – Paradise Wood

Normally trees are felled when they are about fifty to sixty years old

After felling, the 'brash' is removed and the logs are cut into equal lengths

Deepdale Meadow is enriched by spring water rising from the limestone

Occasionally wetland areas are left unplanted to create diversity of habitat within the forest

Top left: *Cropton Forest*
Bottom left: *Wood anemones by a stream*

The forest has been opened up for recreation – a picnic place at Crosscliffe

Staindale lake

Overleaf: *Occasionally Scots pine are left to reach full maturity, creating an island of naturalness in the forest – Paradise Wood*

An example of wildwood – Keldy

The British Trust for Ornithology works closely with the gamekeeper
monitoring the nesting sites of rarer birds.
Rain and mist provide cover for Wilf Norman while he rings some merlin chicks

Ralph Cross

Left: *A young walker tries out an ancient track or 'trod' near Commondale*

Preparing for the shooting season.
The gamekeeper checks the position of the pegs, which are used as markers for the 'guns' when there are
no butts

A shoot provides a welcome opportunity for local people to come together for a day out beating

The shooting party

Each to his own!
Guns' lunch

Beaters' lunch

The keeper leads his beaters off on another drive

A gun enjoys the autumnal air with his wife

A drive is discussed. The day is a social occasion for the guns as well as the beaters

The end of the day and the beaters unload

Left: *Retrieving the birds.*
Both beaters and guns take advantage of the occasion to work their dogs

As the shooting season draws to a close, the moors revert to harbouring a comfortable number of grouse during the winter

Washing ropes – care of equipment is essential

rock by eddying water may appear to be invulnerable, this unique world is a fragile one and many caves have been irreparably damaged. Muddy feet, the disposing of debris, and the placing of artificial belays all leave their mark. Stalactites are easily broken, crystal pools have been trampled underfoot, and used carbide from the lamps is frequently discarded indiscriminately. In the same way that awareness of environmental concerns is needed above ground, the caves would also benefit from greater sensitivity by those who visit them.

The attraction of the caves is not easy to define. The beauty of the natural rock forms, the myriad of passageways, the strange sensation of being underground, the thrill of descending big shafts, all play their part. The smells of rock and earth, the sounds of water dripping, gurgling, and rushing downstream through an enclosed cavern, create an experience that is unlike any found above ground. Some would say that the element of risk is also part of the attraction, though others would claim that the lure of danger lies not in courting it, but in using one's knowledge, skill and experience to overcome it.

The world of caves still provides one of the few places on earth where new discoveries can be made. An enthusiast pushes his way along a tight, muddy, flood-prone passage always in the hope that he will break out into an underground river passage, or emerge in a grotto glistening white with formations. Many of the discoveries now being made are through cave divers exploring the flooded passageways or sumps; large systems have been linked together and new caverns found. It is a world that is still opening up, revealing itself to those who respond to its call. It holds numberless secrets and hides both beauty and diversity in its depths. New generations of cavers in years to come will do as others have done before them, and attempt to unravel the untold mysteries of this underworld.

Right: *The Main Stream Passage in Lancaster Hole is a vadose canyon 60 feet high*

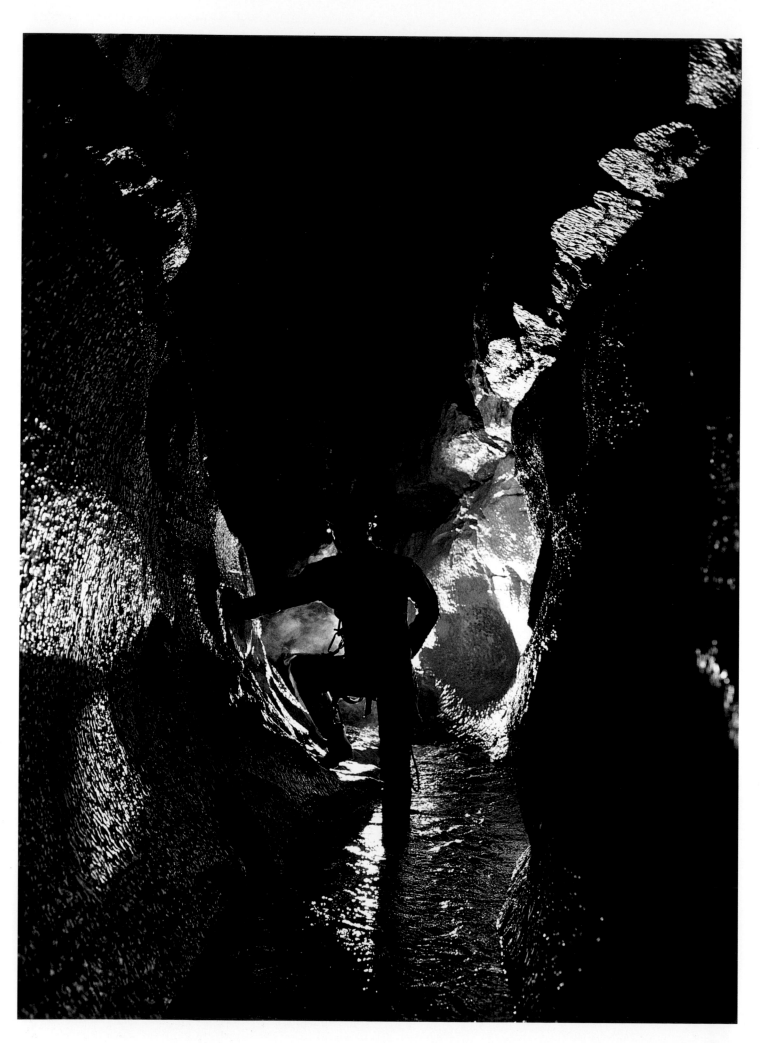

Notts Pot

*The underground streams cut and carve their passage through the rock, working their way even deeper,
leaving behind a complex series of caves and potholes.*
Left: *Kingsdale Master Cave*

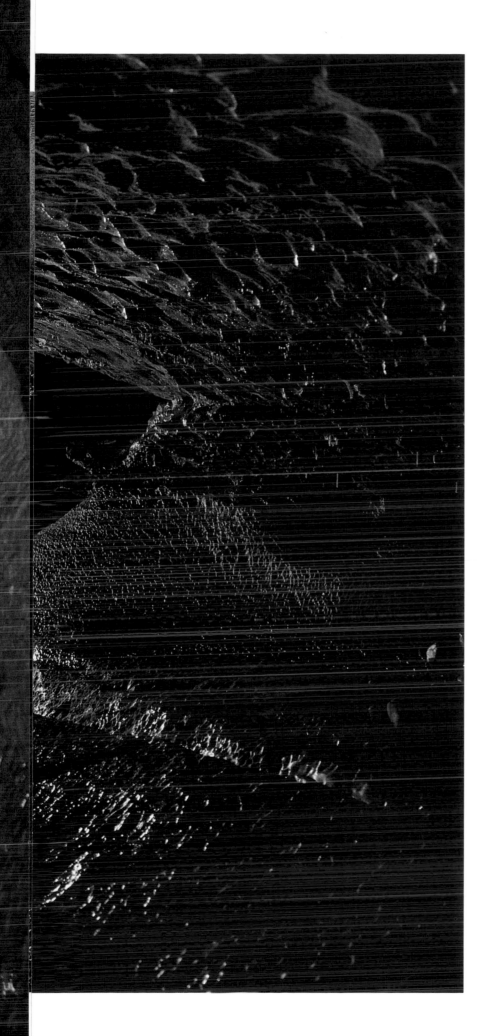

*One of the main attractions of the caves in the Yorkshire Dales is
the remarkable variety of passages and shafts.
A phreatic passage in Ibbeth Peril Cave*

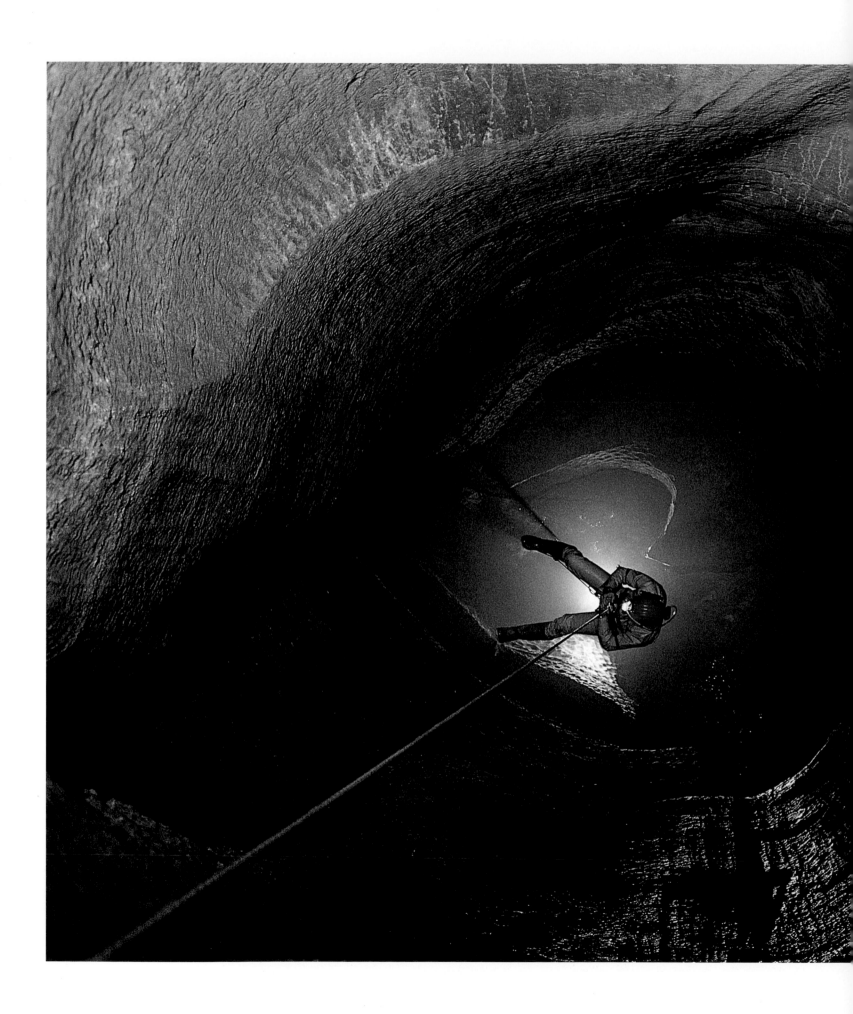

A vadose canyon in Lost John's Hole

An elliptical shaft in Notts Pot

Sometimes the passages are circular in shape – the Roof Tunnel in Kingsdale Master Cave

Right: Shafts vary from narrow slots to open chasms hundreds of feet deep –
a 180 feet pitch in Hurnel Moss Pot

Another attraction of the caves is the formations they contain – a grotto in Gavel Pot

Top right: *Straw stalactites decorate a ceiling in Hagg Gill Pot*
Bottom right: *A secluded chamber with stalagmites in Lancaster Hole is
appropriately named Cape Kennedy*

A caver pauses to admire stalagmites in Pippikin Pot

Top left: *Occasionally calcite is deposited in such a way that it forms a curtain – Pippikin Pot*
Bottom left: *Helictites in King Pot appear to defy gravity as they twist and turn
in convoluted growth*

Overleaf: *It is the thrill of adventure that lures most cavers underground.
Climbing a cascade in Cigalère Inlet, Pippikin Pot*

Cavers often have to negotiate crawls and squeezes – Swinsto Hole

Right: *Rigging pitches is an art in itself. Having abseiled 90 feet down a shaft, a caver safeguards himself by using a traverse line before descending a further 100 feet beneath the Y-anchor*

Previous page: *Abseiling down a sunbeam!*

Active streamways are among the most popular features of Dales caves – Kingsdale Master Cave

Left: *Negotiating a traverse in Diccan Pot in order to rig a pitch away from a waterfall*

A cascade in Ibbeth Peril Cave

Carbide lamps provide the most effective means of lighting underground.
A caver pauses to refill his lamp from an underground pool

Although caving is primarily a sport for adults, some of the easier caves can be enjoyed by children under proper supervision . . . and they often get on better in the squeezes! Long Churn Cave

Right: An experienced caver prepares to descend a 175 feet pitch – Juniper Gulf

Heavy rain can make the easiest of caves tricky and dangerous – Browgill Cave

Left: *Extra care is always needed on a wet pitch*

One of the most frequent problems for the Cave Rescue Organisation is how to reach people trapped underground by flood water – a rescue at Ibbeth Peril Cave

Rescuers use sandbags to divert water away from the cave

Right: *After twenty hours underground, a flood victim is helped to the surface by C.R.O. members*

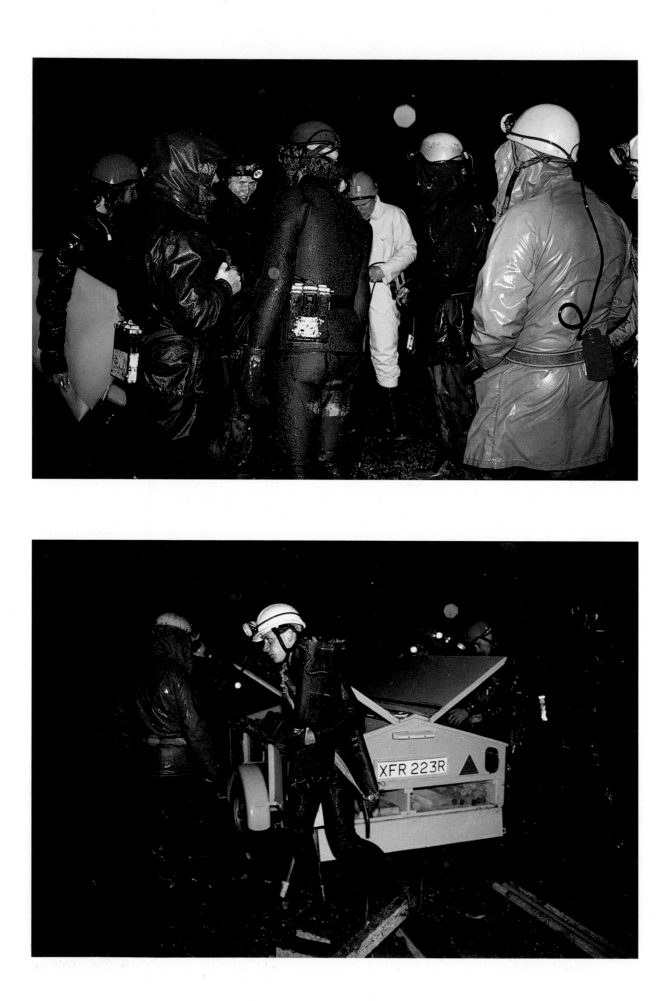

A surface team ensures that food and hot drinks are available for the rescue workers

Left: Whatever the weather or time of day, the C.R.O. members turn out voluntarily to help people who are in trouble

The 'mole phone' enables communication to take place, through solid rock, from passages deep underground to the surface

Left: After falling nearly 80 feet in Simpson's Pot, a caver is brought to safety. Negotiating pitches with a stretcher is physically gruelling work and requires many helpers

On the way out of Alum Pot

Right: *Alum Pot at night*
Overleaf: *Emerging into the sunlight from Browgill Cave*

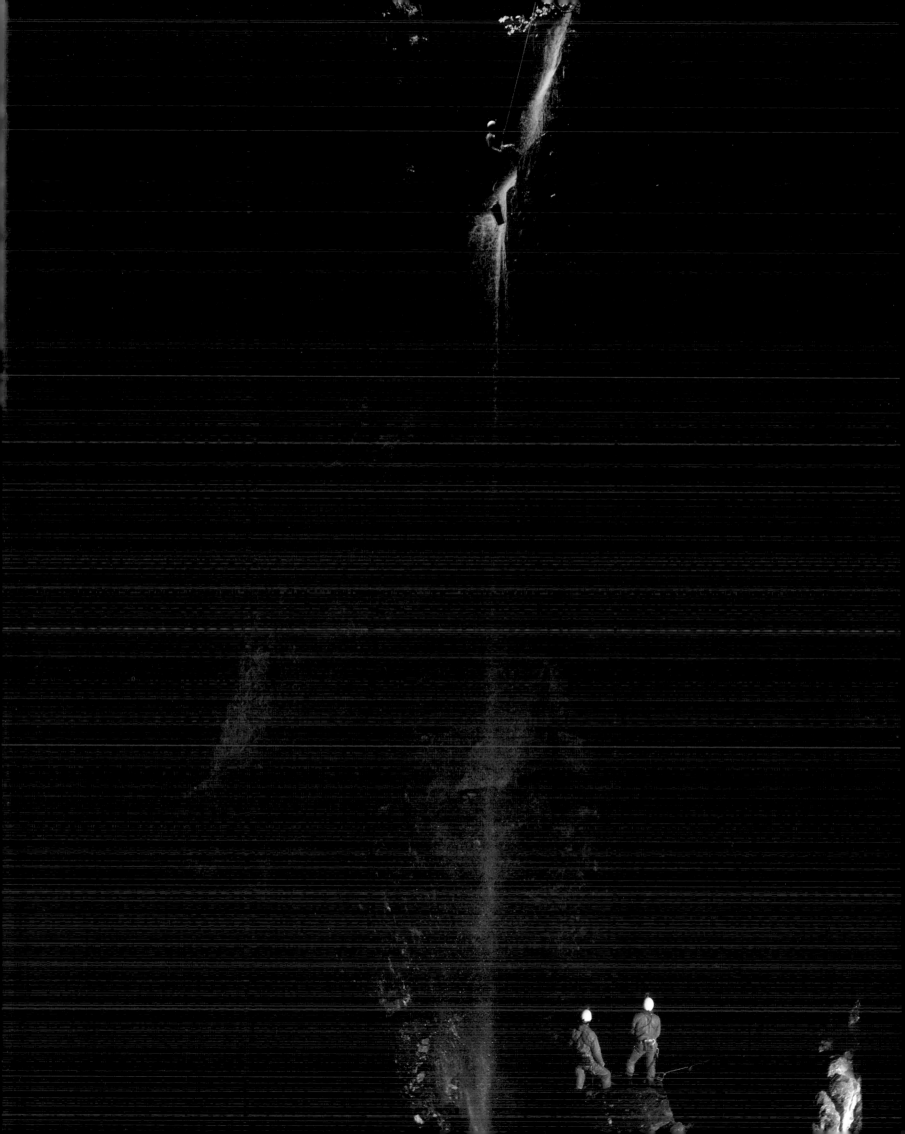

Photographic Notes

The idea for this book was to contrast the wide, open landscape of the North York Moors with the hidden world of caves beneath the Yorkshire Dales. Naturally both stories required completely different photographic techniques. As usual our main concern on the moors was to portray the life as well as the landscape, which this time entailed working with gamekeepers, foresters and farmers, and also going along on a couple of grouse shoots.

Above ground, it was the grouse shoots that seemed to be the most challenging photographically – for they could be pretty scary! One of us accompanied the beaters while the other remained hidden in a butt with a 'gun', but in either case it proved difficult to get good pictures. To get a beater in the same frame as birds flying up, or a 'gun' with birds flying at him, was more a matter of good luck than anything else.

Our medium format cameras have waist level viewfinders, so when we were in the butt we had to stand up in order to see anything through them. Needless to say we quickly resorted to using 35mm, which meant we could keep our heads down lower while a drive was on! We concluded that it is not easy to obtain good shots of a shoot without risking getting shot oneself – though the shooting party were very hospitable and kind and made every effort to help us in whatever way they could!

On these occasions we used fast film, Fujichrome 400 or Kodachrome 200, so as to avoid getting blurred birds. But when photographing the rest of the story on the open moor, we reverted to using our Mamiya 645 cameras and Fujichrome 100 film whenever possible. The only exception to this was in the forest when we found ourselves working in dark and sometimes breezy conditions. Again, faster shutter speeds became a priority.

Photographing underground was a very different story. Caves in the Dales are cold, wet and sometimes muddy places, and these inhospitable conditions conspire to try the patience of the most dedicated cave photogra-

pher. Scrupulous preparation for a trip is essential – rallying helpers, charging up flashguns, packing caving gear, checking and re-checking camera equipment to make sure nothing is forgotten. When underground, the simplest task becomes a trial – even communicating with one another! When a stream is flowing underground or a waterfall is crashing down nearby, the noise echoes around preventing any chance of normal speech. When the photographer is at the top of a pitch and the caver at the bottom, the only way of relaying instructions is by means of coded whistles.

Protecting cameras and flashguns is of vital importance. Carrying expensive gear through wet passageways, narrow crawls and up and down shafts means that it has to be well padded as well as completely water proofed. Ex-army ammunition boxes have been used for many years and have proved safe and popular, but they are heavy and cumbersome. Although we did take our medium format cameras underground on several occasions, we often resorted to using 35mm gear as it is less bulky. For the most part we used Kodachrome 200 which, when used with electronic flash, we found gave the best results.

In addition to the cameras, three or four different flashguns, slave units, connecting leads, cable release, spare batteries and tripod were also included. A 'slave' is an essential piece of equipment when two people are working alone underground, as it has the facility of firing a flashgun remotely. It does this by means of a 'magic eye' which intercepts light from one flashgun to fire the other. This enabled us to set up shots using different lighting combinations without always having to rely on extra helpers.

Each passage, formation, chamber and waterfall needs lighting in a different way, and it is the skill of the cave photographer to use the right combination of side or back lighting to achieve the most dramatic effect. The simplest way to take a photograph underground is to clip a flashgun onto the camera and fire away. Unfortunately this

invariably results in dull, flat, boring pictures. Getting the flashgun away from the camera, by even a metre or so, immediately improves the result. But that is when the complications begin!

As soon as the simplest lead is introduced between camera and flashgun, moisture insidiously seeps into the connections, causing short-circuits and misfires. And when setting up flashguns and slave units on ledges in different parts of a streamway to achieve more complex effects, providence is truly tempted. To take a picture when everything works as planned appears as a miracle. Mud, grit, water and damp atmosphere are not compatible with electronic equipment, and patience and good humour become as vital a part of the procedure as taking plenty of spare film.

Apart from equipment failure there are other problems too. When a specific photograph is set up, it is often too dark to see much through the viewfinder, which makes it not only difficult to decide on the best camera position, but also awkward to focus. For these reasons it is obviously much easier to take a photograph of a static subject rather than to organize an action shot. When photographing a decorated grotto there is time and space to try out alternative lighting combinations to gain the best effect. When photographing a big pitch, a willing helper may be asked to hang on a rope for three quarters of an

hour while flashes are fired from top and bottom and different apertures are tried! Meanwhile the photographer always has to remain concerned about his own safety.

To photograph the underground world is similar to lighting a stage set: the photographer is completely dependent on artificial light and has to create his own effects. Yet, underground, the final result always has to be imagined and envisaged for it can never be seen beforehand. But there lies the challenge and also the fulfilment.

There is no doubt that we could not have worked on this project without the help of other experienced cavers. Dave Shearsmith gave up numerous weekends and holidays to immerse himself in waterfalls, get numb with cold, prusik up hundreds of feet of rope and spend hours in streamways of diverse shapes and sizes. As a competent caver with an interest in photography, he made an ideal companion for John, and saved Eliza from going on many of the harder trips that she did not fancy! Both of us are deeply grateful to him for all the help he has given us.

Other caving friends we would like to mention are Chris Stone, Andrew Bradley and Nigel Ball who all accompanied us on photographic trips. Jack Pickup and the C.R.O. kept us informed of incidents and allowed John the freedom to photograph while rescues were in operation. To all these people we are indebted, for without them we could not have made this book.